# America's Civil War

## by L. L. Owens

**Perfection Learning®**

# About the Author

Lisa L. Owens grew up in the Midwest. She studied English and journalism at the University of Iowa. She currently works as an editor in Seattle.

Other books by Ms. Owens include *Abraham Lincoln: A Great American Life* and *A Pirate Tale*.

**Cover and Book Design:** Alan D. Stanley
**Illustration:** Alan D. Stanley pp. 9 (bottom), 33 (bottom), 52

**Image credits:** Tria Giovan/Corbis cover (background image), Bettmann/Corbis p. 38

Art Today pp. 2, 4, 5, 7, 8, 12, 15, 17, 19, 23, 26, 27, 28 (top), 32, 33 (top), 34 (top), 35, 36 (top), 39, 42, 51, 54, back cover (top); Library of Congress pp. 6, 9 (top), 10, 11, 12 (top), 16, 18, 20, 21, 24, 25, 28 (bottom), 29, 30, 31, 34 (bottom), 36 (bottom), 37, 41, 47, 48; Digital Stock pp. cover, 22, 50; National Archives and Records Administration pp. 43, 46; IMSI MasterPhotos back cover (background image)

# Contents

# Setting the Scene

During 1860 and 1861, 11 Southern states left, or seceded from, the United States. They didn't like President Abraham Lincoln's ideas. So they decided to form their own nation.

The new nation was called the Confederate States of America. Richmond, Virginia, was its capital.

Lincoln didn't want the North and the South to separate. He wanted them to stay one strong nation.

The interior of Fort Sumter

But the Southern states didn't agree. They decided to show Lincoln that they were serious.

On April 12, 1861, they attacked Fort Sumter in South Carolina.

Lincoln was left with no choice. He rounded up an army. And he declared war—America's Civil War. It was the only way he could think of to save the Union.

Here are some other common names for the Civil War.

- War Between Brothers
- War Between the North and the South
- War Between the States
- War of Northern Aggression
- War of the Rebellion

Lincoln planned to force the Confederacy to come back to the Union. At first, he even promised not to end slavery if the North won the war.

But on New Year's Day 1863, Lincoln approved the Emancipation Proclamation. This ended slavery. Now ending slavery was an official goal of the war.

The Civil War lasted four long years. More than 600,000 soldiers died.

On April 9, 1865, Confederate General Robert E. Lee *surrendered*. This meant that he admitted defeat.

**Lincoln said—**
"Government cannot endure permanently half slave, half free."

The North had won. Slavery ended. And the states were together again.

# American Life in the Mid-1800s

**Common jobs:** Farmer, chimney sweep, blacksmith, coachman, match girl, peddler, ice cutter, street vendor, cobbler, seamstress, tailor, liveryman, tinker, servant

**Transportation:** Horse, horse-drawn carriage, stagecoach, train, ship

**Light sources:** Gaslights, candles, kerosene lamps, lard-oil lamps

**Popular songs:** "The Battle Hymn of the Republic," "Camptown Races," "Polly Wolly Doodle," "Oh! Susannah," "When Johnny Comes Marching Home Again"

**Common foods:** Chipped beef, turkey, chicken, gumbo, macaroni, beans, corn bread, pickles, bacon and collard greens, pretzels, flapjacks, sweet potato pie, apple dumplings, peanut brittle, cherry pie, apple cider, tea, coffee

**Favorite pastimes:** Baseball games, dances, billiards, circuses, boxing matches, dogfights, checkers, horse races, sleigh rides, theater plays

8

# A Civil War Timeline

**1860**

Hannibal
Hamlin

- Abraham Lincoln is elected president of the United States. Hannibal Hamlin is vice president.

- Seven states secede from the Union: South Carolina, Mississippi, Florida, Alabama, Georgia, Louisiana, and Texas.

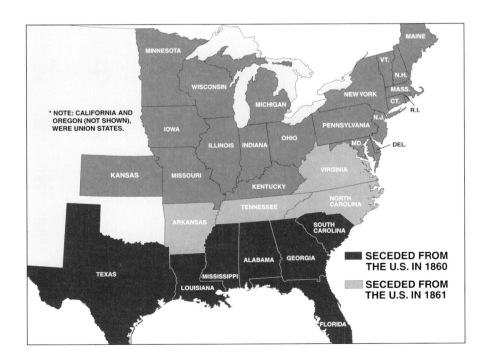

**1861**

- Southern troops attack Fort Sumter.
- Virginia, Arkansas, Tennessee, and North Carolina secede.

Jefferson Davis

- Richmond, Virginia, is named the Confederate capital.
- Jefferson Davis becomes the Confederate president. Alexander Stephens is vice president.
- The Confederacy wins the First Battle of Bull Run.

**1862**

- The Union captures Fort Henry and Fort Donelson.

General
Philip Sheridan

- Philip Sheridan leads the Shenandoah Campaign.
- The Union wins the Battle of Shiloh.
- The Confederacy wins the Second Battle of Bull Run.
- The September 17 battle at Antietam is grim. The Union wins.

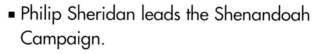

**10**

**1863**

- Lincoln signs the Emancipation Proclamation. This frees all slaves in Confederate territories.
- The Union is defeated at Chancellorsville.
- The Union wins at Gettysburg.
- Lincoln delivers the Gettysburg Address.
- Union forces win at Chattanooga.

**1864**

- The Union attacks Richmond.

Andrew Johnson

- Northern troops march from Tennessee to Georgia. Sherman's men capture Atlanta.
- Lincoln is elected to a second term. Andrew Johnson is vice president.

General Sherman after capturing Atlanta

**11**

**1865**

- General Lee surrenders at Appomattox Court House.

- Lincoln is shot and killed while watching a play. Vice President Andrew Johnson becomes president.

- The 13th Amendment is ratified. Slavery ends in the U.S.

# Chapter 1

# What Was Life Like?

## For Southerners

Most people in the South were poor. And most lived on farms. Cotton, tobacco, rice, and corn were the main crops.

The big farms were *plantations*. Rich white families owned them. They used slaves to plant and harvest their huge crops.

About 10,000 plantation owners had 50 or more slaves each. A few wealthy men owned as many as 200.

Southerners thought the government was unfair. They were upset by the taxes they had to pay. So they wanted to break away from the Union. That's why Southern states began to secede.

---

### The Confederate States of America
In all, 11 states seceded from the Union. They were

- Alabama
- Arkansas
- Florida
- Georgia
- Louisiana
- Mississippi
- North Carolina
- South Carolina
- Tennessee
- Texas
- Virginia

There were 9 million people in the Confederate states.

---

The South wanted to be free from the North. They wanted **states' rights**. So they created their own nation. It was called the Confederate States of America (C.S.A.).

**States' rights** meant that each state could decide what was right for its people and make laws accordingly.

They elected Jefferson Davis president. Alexander Stephens was his vice president.

Alexander Stephens

A committee wrote a Confederate constitution. It was much the same as the U.S. Constitution. But it left out words about "the general welfare" of the people. It also gave citizens the right to own slaves.

C.S.A. started an army. They talked with U.S. government officials. They wanted the U.S. to accept their new nation.

The two sides could not agree.

## For Northerners

The North was made up of cities, small towns, and rural areas. Some people worked in factories. Others lived in the country. They were farmers.

During the war, there were 23 states in the Union. There were 20 million people.

Children in the North went to public schools. Some helped support their families by working.

Life was hard. But the war created jobs. Farmers fed the troops. Factories built weapons and made uniforms.

Most Northerners thought slavery was wrong. About 250,000 freed slaves lived in the North. Many had escaped from the South.

Black people had a better life in the North than in the South. But they weren't treated as equals. They got the lowest paying jobs. And they were the poorest group.

Northerners did not think of Southerners as their enemies. They did not want to fight them. They felt they were all part of the same nation. And the North wanted it to stay that way.

## For Slaves

A Dutch slave ship had arrived in America in 1619. It landed at Jamestown, Virginia. On it were hundreds of people from Africa.

They had been taken from their homes. Then they'd been forced onto the ship.

They were chained and made to lie flat. They traveled across the sea like that. Many died during the long trip.

This began the slave trade in America. It lasted until 1863.

In 1775, slavery was legal. People in all 13 colonies owned slaves.

By 1860, slaves had been escaping to the North for 30 years. People in the North no longer used slave labor. They had come to see that "owning" another human being was wrong.

But 4 million slaves still worked in the South. They did all the hard labor. Their white owners kept the profits.

Some slaves worked in a master's main house. They cooked and cleaned for his family.

## The Brutal Treatment of Slaves

Slaves were treated like animals or worse.

- The law didn't recognize slaves' marriages.
- Their children could not go to school.
- Slaves' homes were crowded and dirty.
- They had little food.
- They had little or no money.
- They could be sold to a new owner at any time.
- Sometimes babies were taken from parents and sold.
- Slaves had no freedom or rights. They had to do whatever white people said. If they didn't, they were punished harshly.
- Some were whipped. Some were beaten. And many were killed.

When a plantation owner died, his property was divided or sold. That included slaves. They were put up for sale. They were treated like the furniture and the sheep or cows.

A strong male slave cost as much as $2,000. That was a huge amount of money in the 1860s.

**19**

In the North, most free blacks worked as servants and laborers. They usually worked for whites.

They were not allowed to own land. They could not own a gun. And they were still treated as "less than equal" to whites. This continued long after the Civil War.

Still, life in the North was much better than life as a slave.

About 200,000 free black men fought for the Union. They fought bravely. They wanted to end slavery.

There were 60 all-black units in the Union. By the end of the war, 1 out of every 8 Union soldiers was black.

Slavery ended for good in America in 1865.

# Chapter 2

# Great Leaders

★ **Fighting for the Union** ★

## General Ulysses S. Grant

Grant was a Civil War hero. He led Union forces to victory. And he was respected for his great courage.

President Lincoln made Grant general in chief in March 1864. He led all the Union armies.

**21**

In June 1864, he faced General Lee at Richmond. Grant had to withdraw his troops.

Grant would later accept Lee's surrender. That happened on April 9, 1865, at Appomattox Court House, Virginia.

Grant went on to become the 18th president of the United States.

Later, he made many poor business decisions. His final years were spent in poverty. To support his family, Grant sold items he'd saved from the war. Then he wrote a book about his life.

The book was very successful. But Grant died before he could see the profits.

Appomattox Court House

# General William T. Sherman

Sherman was a skilled Union general. He helped win many early battles.

Many thought he was brilliant. They also thought he was a bit **mad**.

Once he demanded 200,000 men for one battle. To that, Commander George McClellan said,"Sherman is gone in the head."

**Mad** means "insane" or "not using good judgement."

Sherman was quickly moved away from the major part of the war. But his great battle skills impressed General Grant. And he was moved back to the front.

He was wounded at the Battle of Shiloh. But he refused to leave the battlefield. He fought to the finish.

In 1864, Sherman led a 100,000-man attack on Atlanta. He later sent a telegraph to President Lincoln. It read

Atlanta is ours—and fairly won.

His troops then began the March to the Sea. They destroyed property, supplies, livestock—anything in their way. Their path, which led them to Savannah, was 300 miles long. And 60 miles wide.

Sherman wrote

War is cruelty. There is no use trying to reform it. The crueler it is, the sooner it will be over.

Shell-damaged house in Atlanta

# General Philip H. Sheridan

During the war, Sheridan was in his early 30s. He was one of the youngest leaders in the Civil War.

He showed the enemy no mercy. He led his cavalry unit through the South. The men in the cavalry rode horses.

They drove people from their homes. Then they burned down the houses.

"Smash 'em up! Smash 'em up!" Sheridan cried.

His most famous attacks were in the Shenandoah Valley. For seven months, he led 40,000 troops through Virginia. He put what he called his "scorched earth" policy into effect. Much of the valley was burned and left in ruins.

# Sheridan at Cedar Creek

Herman Melville was a famous author. He wrote the book *Moby Dick*. He also wrote some Civil War poetry.

One of his poems was about General Sheridan. It's called "Sheridan at Cedar Creek." It was written in October 1864. And it's about Sheridan at battle.

Here's the first verse.

Shoe the steed with silver
That bore him to the fray,
When he heard the guns at dawning—
Miles away;
When he heard them calling, calling—
Mount! nor stay:
Quick, or all is lost;
They've surprised and stormed the post.
They push your routed host—
Gallop! retrieve the day.

# General George G. Meade

Meade led troops at Bull Run, Antietam, Chancellorsville, and Gettysburg. He was commander of the Army of the Potomac.

Meade was overjoyed when General Lee gave up. A soldier reported that Meade rode "like mad down the road with his hat off."

As he rode, Meade shouted, "The war is over! And we are going home!"

Generals of the Army of the Potomac: Governor K. Warren, William H. French, George G. Meade, Henry J. Hunt, Andrew A. Humphreys, John Sedgwick

# General Robert E. Lee

Lee was a native of Virginia. His father was a Revolutionary War hero.

Lee did not believe in slavery. And he agreed with President Lincoln. He wanted the nation to stay united.

Lincoln offered Lee the command of the Union Army.

Lee was very loyal, though. He felt a sense of duty to his home state. So he turned Lincoln down.

He said, "I cannot raise my hand against my birthplace, my home, my children."

He joined Confederate forces a few days later.

A friend said, "He will take more chances, and take them quicker, than any other general in this country. North or South."

Lee helped the South win several great battles.

## General Thomas Jonathan "Stonewall" Jackson

Jackson was a good friend of General Lee. He was one of the army's most popular leaders. He was also a highly skilled leader.

He was a hero at the Battles of Bull Run and Chancellorsville. Union troops were unable to get past him.

Once a soldier said, "There is Jackson. He is standing like a stone wall." And that's how he got the nickname "Stonewall."

In 1862, Jackson was shot. It was dusk. His own men had opened fire on him. It was a tragic mistake.

It seemed that he would recover from his wounds. But then he came down with **pneumonia**. He died several days later.

**Pneumonia** is an infection of the lungs.

## General Nathan B. Forrest

Forrest was a fierce cavalry commander.

Forrest's unit won many battles. He was wounded four times. And 30 horses were shot from under him.

His motto was

Get there first with the most men.

He usually did.

General Sherman saw Forrest as a real threat. He wanted him dead. He said it was worth it. Even if it "costs 10,000 lives and breaks the treasury."

In April 1864, Forrest's men killed more than 300 former slaves in battle.

He surrendered his troops in May 1865.

## General Pierce G. T. Beauregard

Beauregard joined the Confederate army in early 1861. Soon he led the attack upon Fort Sumter.

He planned much of the First Battle of Bull Run. He bravely took over at the Battle of Shiloh when his commander died.

Beauregard also designed the Confederacy's "Southern Cross" battle flag.

# General James Ewell Brown "Jeb" Stuart

Stuart served under General Lee. He was a brave cavalryman.

He led his men on many important scouting missions.

He provided Lee with information about Union troops. He told Lee where the enemy was and what they were planning to do next.

Lee called Stuart "the eyes and ears of my army."

President Jefferson Davis, General Robert E. Lee and other Confederate Army generals

# Chapter 3

# Remarkable Women

Countless women supported the war effort. They were from both sides. Many opened their homes to hungry and wounded soldiers. Some were nurses. Others were spies.

About 400 women disguised themselves as men. Why? So they could fight on the battlefields themselves!

Here are just some of those women.

## Louisa May Alcott

Alcott worked as a Civil War nurse. She later wrote a book about it. It was called *Hospital Sketches*.

She was also active in politics. She was the first woman to register to vote in Concord.

# Clara Barton

After the Second Battle of Bull Run, Barton created an agency. Its purpose was to give supplies to wounded soldiers.

Barton visited the most dangerous battlefields. She helped soldiers of both the North and South. She was known as the "Angel of the Battlefield."

At Antietam, a Confederate bullet shot through her sleeve. It killed the soldier she was helping.

After the war, Barton became a popular speaker. She established the American Red Cross in 1881.

-Nurses of America-
humanity
calls you

what is your answer?
enroll now with the American Red Cross for Army or Navy service

# Dr. Elizabeth Blackwell

Blackwell was the head of a volunteer group. It gave donations to Union soldiers. The group later became the U.S. Sanitary Commission.

# Rosie O'Neal Greenhow

Greenhow was a leader in Washington society. She supported secession. And she was one of the most noted spies in the Civil War.

# Sojourner Truth

Truth was a former slave. She escaped to freedom in the 1820s.

Her given name was Isabella Baumfree. She changed it when she dedicated her life to public speaking. Her mission was to "travel up and down the land" spreading the truth about the horrors of slavery.

Truth also spoke out for women's right to vote.

# Harriet Tubman

Tubman was an escaped slave. She risked her life for her freedom. Then she risked it many more times to help others.

Her nickname was "Moses." She led hundreds of slaves on a secret "path" to freedom.

The path was the Underground Railroad. It was a series of tunnels, roads, and homes. It led to the safety of the North.

During the war, Tubman worked for the Union army. She served as a spy, a scout, and a nurse.

Harriet Tubman (far left) with a group of former slaves that she helped escape to freedom

# Loreta Velazquez

Velazquez was the widow of a Confederate soldier. She disguised herself as a man. She took the name Harry Buford.

It worked. People thought she was a man. She fought in many battles.

Eventually, someone discovered she was a woman. Then she became a spy for the South. She once wrote

> I was as good a soldier as any man around me, and as willing as any to fight valiantly and to the bitter end . . .

# Dr. Mary Edwards Walker

Walker was a surgeon. She tended to wounded soldiers.

She was captured in the South. She was a prisoner of war for four months.

Walker later received the Medal of Honor. Congress awarded it to her for her bravery.

# War by the Numbers

Many lives were lost during the Civil War. It was a sad time in U.S. history. Americans killed other Americans. Some family members even fought against each other.

Here are some facts. They show the reality of what happened on the battlefields.

- About 3 million soldiers fought during the Civil War.

- Some sources say that 624,511 soldiers died in the Civil War. American deaths in all other wars combined have been about 650,000.

- About 62% of the deaths during the war were caused by disease.

- Some 70% of the soldiers were under 23 years of age. About 10% were 16 or younger.

- Of the 6,500 Confederate soldiers in the First Battle of Bull Run, 387 died.

- Of the 11,000 Union soldiers at the First Battle of Bull Run, 460 died.

- At the Second Battle of Bull Run, 55,000 Confederate troops defeated 75,000 Union troops.

- More than 51,000 soldiers were killed, wounded, or captured at Gettysburg.

View of the battlefield at Bull Run, Virginia

- The 26th North Carolina Regiment lost 588 soldiers at Gettysburg. That was more than half of the regiment.

- The Union's 24th Michigan Regiment lost 4 out of every 5 men at Gettysburg.

- At Gettysburg, 1 out of every 5 Union soldiers died.

- At Gettysburg, 1 out of every 3 Confederate soldiers died.

- During a riot, 120 New York citizens, including children, died. People were protesting the draft.

- At Cold Harbor, 7,000 Union soldiers died in 20 short minutes.

- At the Battle of Petersburg, the First Maine Artillery Regiment lost 210 out of 1,200 men.

- During Pickett's Charge, the Confederate Virginia Brigade lost 941 men out of 1,427.

- Each side took 200,000 prisoners of war. About 1 in every 7 died in prison.

- At the end of the war, 50,000 soldiers went home with missing limbs.

An amputation being performed at a Gettysburg hospital tent

# Chapter 5

# A Soldier's Vocabulary

Here are some weapons, supplies, and terms seen and heard on the battlefield.

**artillery**          large weapons, such as the cannons

**bayonet**          an 18-inch blade attached to the front end of a rifle

**bedroll**          blankets rolled and carried by soldiers

| | |
|---|---|
| **bully soup** | hot cereal eaten by Union soldiers |
| **bummer** | a soldier who took what he needed from farmers and townspeople |
| **canteen** | a tin or wood container on a strap. Soldiers carried liquid in it. |
| **cap** | a small device used to explode powder in a musket barrel |
| **cartridge** | a paper tube. It held a bullet and gunpowder. |
| **cavalry** | a group of men who fought on horseback |
| **copperhead** | a person from the North who sided with the South |
| **federals** | another name for the Union soldiers |

**hardtack**    a dry, hard, stale biscuit made out of flour, salt, and water. Union soldiers ate them often. The biscuits were also called "worm castles" and "teeth dullers."

**haversack**    a small canvas sack. Soldiers carried food in it.

**housewife**    a small sewing kit

**infantry**    a group of men who fought on foot

**ironclad**    an iron fighting ship

**Johnny Reb**    a nickname for a Confederate soldier

**kepi**    a cap worn by Confederate soldiers

**knapsack**    a canvas container strapped to the back. A soldier carried personal belongings in it.

**mess**    a group of 5–20 men who ate, worked, and fought together

Quaker guns at Confederate winter headquarters in Centreville, Virginia

**Quaker guns**     fake cannons. The Confederates used them to fool the enemy.

**Rebel**     a Confederate soldier

**Rebel yell**     a Confederate war cry

**rifled-musket**     a muzzle-loading gun

**suspenders**     cloth or leather bands used to hold up pants

**Yankee**     a nickname for a Union soldier

# Chapter 6

# Two Crucial Battles

## Antietam

*September 17, 1862*

General Lee was eager for the South to score another victory. They had just won the Second Battle of Bull Run.

Lee's forces prepared for battle. They were just outside Sharpsburg, Maryland. The men lined up along Antietam Creek.

The fighting began at 6 A.M. There were 75,000 Union troops. General George McClellan was in charge.

Lee had just 40,000 men.

About 27,000 men were killed in 12 hours. Each side lost about the same number of troops.

In the end, Lee was forced to retreat. His men were outnumbered.

The battle is known as the Bloodiest Day in U.S. military history.

President Lincoln was pleased with this Union win. He saw it as a turning point.

President Lincoln on the battlefield of Antietam

# Gettysburg
## *July 1, 1863*

A Confederate cavalry unit rode into Gettysburg, Pennsylvania. They were hoping to get a new supply of shoes. Instead, they were spotted by Union troops. The battle began.

The Battle of Gettysburg lasted three days. The Confederates won the first day. But the Union had defeated them by the third.

The Confederates knew that Union forces were stronger. So they retreated. They were tired. And they had run out of food.

Some say that the Union could have continued to attack. They probably would have won. And the war might have ended.

But Union troops were also tired. They had fought hard. They let the Confederates retreat.

The war went on for two more years.

Many men died at Gettysburg. On November 19, 1863, the nation honored them. A cemetery was created on the battlefield. About 15,000 people attended the dedication ceremony.

Edward Everett gave a long, heartfelt speech. People sang a hymn for the dead. And President Lincoln gave the Gettysburg Address. That speech remains one of the most popular speeches in American history.

... nation,

For bro conceived in liberty and dedicated to the proposition that all men are created equal. Now we are engaged in a great civil war, testing whether that nation or any nation so conceived and so dedicated can long endure. We are met on a great battlefield of that war. We have come to dedicate a portion of that field as a final ting-place for those who here gave their lives ight live. It is altogether ld do this. But

# Chapter 7

# The End of the War

## April 9, 1865

Confederate troops lined up at dawn. It was time for battle. The men positioned themselves west of the Appomattox village.

Union soldiers were stationed in front of the Confederate line. They had a row of cannons and trenches.

The Union line opened cannon fire. Then the Confederate attack signal was sounded.

The Confederates marched forward. They cried out the Rebel yell.

Confederates advanced from 7 A.M. to 9 A.M. Then they retreated.

Lee received an urgent message. His troops could no longer go forward. The only thing he could do was surrender. He sent a truce flag to General Sheridan.

Later, Generals Lee and Grant met in the McLean House. They agreed to the terms of surrender. And they signed the official papers.

Lee passed his men on his way to his headquarters. Tears streamed down his face. He said, "Men, we have fought through the war together. I have done the best that I could for you."

The Civil War was finally over.

# Bibliography

There is so much to learn about the Civil War. Here are some great books to look for.

*Abraham Lincoln: A Great American Life*
by L. L. Owens

*Across Five Aprils* by Irene Hunt

*Across the Lines* by Carolyn Reeder

*A Battle of the Civil War* by Mary Stolz

*The Boys' War: Confederate and Union Soldiers Talk About the Civil War* by Jim Murphy

*Brothers at War* by L. L. Owens

*Bull Run* by Paul Fleischman

*Charley Skedaddle* by Patricia Beatty

*The Civil War: Moments in History*
by Shirley Jordan

*Code of the Drum* by L. L. Owens

*Daily Life on a Southern Plantation, 1853*
by Paul Erickson

*Follow the Drinking Gourd* by F. N. Monjo

*For Home and Country: A Civil War Scrapbook* by
Angel Bolotin

*Freedom Train* by Dorothy Sterling

*Just a Few Words, Mr. Lincoln* by Jean Fritz

*Learning About Bravery from the Life of Harriet
Tubman* by Kiki Mosher

*Learning About Honesty from the Life of Abraham
Lincoln* by Kiki Mosher

*A Letter for Mr. Lincoln* by Alvin R. Cunningham

*Lightning Time* by Douglas Rees

*Lincoln: A Photobiography* by Russell Freedman

*Pink and Say* by Patricia Polacco

*The Root Cellar* by Janet Lunn

*Shades of Gray* by Carolyn Reeder

*Soldier's Heart* by Gary Paulsen

*Stonewall* by Jean Fritz